Stop the Shop?

by Jenny Alexander

Contents

Introduction   3
The Chairwoman, Mrs Grant

The supermarket spokesperson   6
Mr Robert Reed

The wildlife warden   13
Mr John Belmont

The shopkeeper   16
Mrs Lynn Payne

The townspeople   20

The vote   30

Glossary   32

Introduction

As you all know, Megamart wants to build a big new out-of-town supermarket here in Westbay. Some people think it's a wonderful idea, but others are very unhappy about it. We have called this public meeting tonight to discuss the project.

We are lucky to have a panel of speakers here to talk to us tonight. First, Mr Robert Reed, the **spokesperson** from Megamart, will tell us why we should support the project. Next, Mr John Belmont, the **wildlife warden** from Westbay Meadows, will speak against it. Then Mrs Lynn Payne will speak on behalf of the Westbay shopkeepers. Finally, you in the audience will have a chance to ask questions and offer your own opinions.

The supermarket spokesperson
– Mr Robert Reed

Good evening, ladies and gentlemen. I'm delighted to see that so many people are interested in this project. The new store will bring huge benefits to Westbay. It will be built outside the town, so there won't even be much inconvenience to the public during the building stage.

As you can see from this plan, the new store will offer much more than just wonderful shopping. It will also have a **crèche**, a cafeteria, a dry-cleaning service and customer toilets. There will be plenty of car-parking space, with trees and shrubs. There will also be a petrol station and a **recycling point**.

Some people are unhappy about out-of-town developments. But it would not be possible to build such a wonderful facility *in* the town, because there isn't enough land available, and it would cost too much. Besides, there are lots of reasons why out-of-town shopping is actually better. It helps reduce traffic in the town. There are no big delivery lorries rumbling through town streets and there is less pressure on car-parking space. Less traffic means a safer town centre.

Out-of-town shopping means:
- low prices
- choice
- freshness

Because it is cheaper to build out of town, our prices will be cheaper. We will also offer more choice, because we will have the space to carry a very large **stock**. And because we will sell so much, nothing will stay on the shelf for very long. This means our food will be fresher.

As well as low prices, choice and freshness, there are lots of other reasons why people like out-of-town shopping. There are no parking problems. There is no need to carry a heavy shopping bag. Out-of-town supermarkets are spacious, clean and pleasant. They are also safe and well lit, away from dark streets and busy roads. Finally, they stay open seven days a week, sometimes for fourteen hours a day.

30% shelf-fillers

15% support services – legal team, etc.

5% managers

50% customer services – till, café, bakery, etc

The Westbay store will bring 200 new jobs into an area where there's not much work outside the holiday season. This picture shows the variety of work that will be on offer. More jobs may follow as well, because once the new roads are built to serve the site, it is likely that other businesses will be attracted to the area.

The wildlife warden

– Mr John Belmont

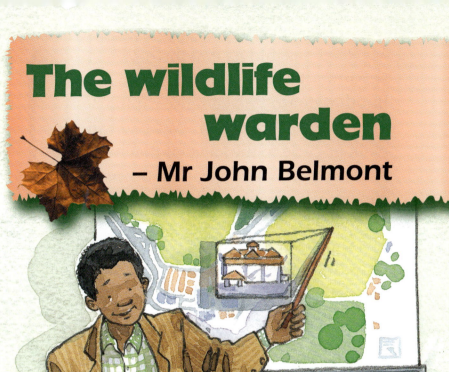

Out-of-town development is bad for the local environment, and I urge you to reject the proposal. We should not be building on **greenfield sites**. We should be protecting the countryside around us. The countryside is not just pretty. It is also vital for our health and well-being. Trees and other plants help to improve the air quality and reduce traffic noise. If we have to have a new supermarket, it should be on a **brownfield site**, like the area where the old station yard was.

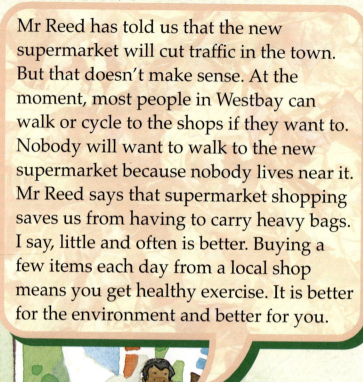

Mr Reed has told us that the new supermarket will cut traffic in the town. But that doesn't make sense. At the moment, most people in Westbay can walk or cycle to the shops if they want to. Nobody will want to walk to the new supermarket because nobody lives near it. Mr Reed says that supermarket shopping saves us from having to carry heavy bags. I say, little and often is better. Buying a few items each day from a local shop means you get healthy exercise. It is better for the environment and better for you.

natterjack toad

great crested newt

coral necklace

In Westbay Meadows, where I am the wildlife warden, we have several pairs of **natterjack toads**. These toads are very rare in Britain now. Unless we protect the places they live in, they will become extinct. There might be other protected species like natterjack toads living on the site where Megamart wants to build. We should not let the development go ahead until we know what lives on the site.

The shopkeeper
– Mrs Lynn Payne

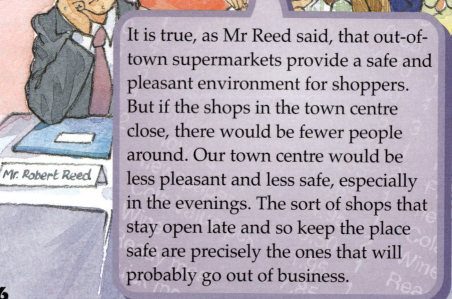

It is true, as Mr Reed said, that out-of-town supermarkets provide a safe and pleasant environment for shoppers. But if the shops in the town centre close, there would be fewer people around. Our town centre would be less pleasant and less safe, especially in the evenings. The sort of shops that stay open late and so keep the place safe are precisely the ones that will probably go out of business.

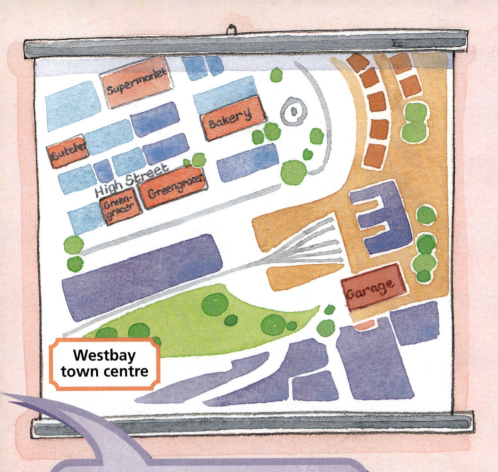

Westbay town centre

Here is a map of the town centre. The shops that are highlighted in red are all likely to close if the Megamart store is built. You can see they include a bakery, two greengrocers, a butchers, a garage and our own small supermarket in the High Street. You will not be able to buy a loaf of bread or a carton of milk without getting in the car.

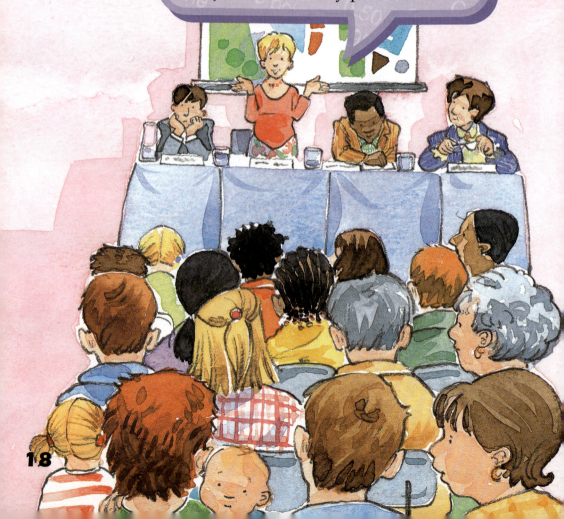

As well as the shops in the town centre, there are three general stores in villages outside Westbay that will be under pressure if this supermarket goes ahead. These village shops are a lifeline for poorer people, old people and people who can't drive. They also provide a meeting-place for people who live alone.

The townspeople

My name is Adam Stone, and I own the Seaview Caravan Park. I find my visitors are surprised and disappointed that there isn't a proper supermarket here. They expect to have the same **goods and services** on holiday as they are used to having at home.

But that's not the same thing at all. We don't go shopping just to get our groceries. We go to meet other people. We go to get a bit of fresh air. I don't want to sit at home and wait for my groceries to be delivered. Besides, that would make me feel more helpless. I can do my shopping for myself at the moment, and that's how I want it to stay!

I'm a mother with two small children. Shopping in town is a complete nightmare for me. I have to cope with a double pushchair, as well as carrying bags of shopping. When the children get too big to go in the pushchair, I think it'll be even worse. There's so much traffic on the roads, and the pavements are so crowded. The new supermarket will be fantastic for me.

The vote

"And who doesn't want an out-of-town supermarket?"

"Tourists prefer the old-fashioned feel."

"We need to protect the natural world."

"Older children can use local shops."

"We want to be able to shop for ourselves."

If you lived in Westbay, would you want an out-of-town supermarket?

Glossary

brownfield site — a piece of land that has been used for building in the past

crèche — a safe area where babies and young children are looked after by trained child-care staff

goods and services — things that people buy instead of making or doing them themselves

greenfield site — a piece of land which has never been used for building

natterjack toad — a rare toad with a bright yellow stripe down its back. It has a loud croak, and it moves by running rather than hopping

recycling point — large containers where you can leave old bottles, newspapers and cans, which are then taken away to be used again

spokesperson — a person who speaks on behalf of an organisation

stock — the things the shop sells

wildlife warden — a person who looks after wild plants and animals on a nature reserve